The Mour

are Calling

Written by Brad and Jim Tonner

Illustrated by Brad Tonner

TwinDesigns Gift Shop

8 Central Square Bristol, New Hampshire
www.TwinDesignsGiftShop.com
www.facebook.com/TwinDesigns

ISBN: 1511625244
ISBN-13: 978-1511625241
Library of Congress Control Number: 2015905791
Printed: North Charleston, South Carolina

This book is dedicated to our wonderful friend Bebe Wood who joyously has heard the mountains calling and shared that with so many.

All THE BEST

Jim AND BRAD

Tannck

The Mountains

are Calling

Written by Brad and Jim Tonner

Illustrated by Brad Tonner

Published by The Road Less Traveled Press

The mountains are calling and I must go.

I must go on a mountain bike ride.

I must go camping.

I must go swimming.

I must go skiing.

I must go on a picnic.

I must go on a hike.

I must go fishing.

I must stop and smell the flowers.

I must find a covered bridge.

I must go sledding.

I must find a log cabin.

I must climb my favorite mountain.

I must watch the moon rise above
the mountains.

I must go rock climbing.

I must go snowmobiling.

I must watch for shooting stars.

I must go blueberry picking.

I must go tubing.

I must go on a zip line.

I must go kayaking.

I must go apple picking.

I must buy a gift for a special friend.

I must spend a day having fun.

I must find a moose.

25

I must go sightseeing.

I must go see the leaves change colors.

I must buy some maple syrup.

The mountains are always calling me,
and I must go back again.

29

The mountains have always been calling us.

Brad and Jim Tonner

And they always will.

Made in the USA
Middletown, DE
27 July 2015